2023

A

WONDROUS

YEAR

Weekly Planner by

S.W. Velault

this planner belongs to:

Also by Sze Wing Vetault

Books and Other Products

Goddess with Many Faces

21 Days of Inspiration

Goddess Weekly Planner

Goddess Daily Planner

Wildflowers 2022 Planner

Spring Bloom Journal

Summer Delights Journal

Autumn Magic Journal

Winter Wonders Journal

For more information and free resources, please visit:
www.SzeWingVetault.com

"When a woman decides to be her true self,
she acts from the wisdom of her heart and lives from the
depth of her soul. She transforms the power from her inner
realm to the outer world.

She embodies the essence of a goddess.

She transcends into a wondrous woman."

Szelwing Vetault

2023

2023

January

M	T	W	T	F	S	S
						1
2	3	4	5	6	7	8
9	10	11	12	13	14	15
16	17	18	19	20	21	22
23	24	25	26	27	28	29
30	31					

◯:7 ◑:15 ●:22 ◐:29

February

M	T	W	T	F	S	S
		1	2	3	4	5
6	7	8	9	10	11	12
13	14	15	16	17	18	19
20	21	22	23	24	25	26
27	28					

◯:6 ◑:14 ●:20 ◐:27

March

M	T	W	T	F	S	S
		1	2	3	4	5
6	7	8	9	10	11	12
13	14	15	16	17	18	19
20	21	22	23	24	25	26
27	28	29	30	31		

◯:7 ◑:15 ●:22 ◐:29

April

M	T	W	T	F	S	S
					1	2
3	4	5	6	7	8	9
10	11	12	13	14	15	16
17	18	19	20	21	22	23
24	25	26	27	28	29	30

◯:6 ◑:13 ●:20 ◐:28

May

M	T	W	T	F	S	S
1	2	3	4	5	6	7
8	9	10	11	12	13	14
15	16	17	18	19	20	21
22	23	24	25	26	27	28
29	30	31				

◯:6 ◑:13 ●:20 ◐:28

June

M	T	W	T	F	S	S
			1	2	3	4
5	6	7	8	9	10	11
12	13	14	15	16	17	18
19	20	21	22	23	24	25
26	27	28	29	30		

◯:4 ◑:11 ●:18 ◐:26

July

M	T	W	T	F	S	S
					1	2
3	4	5	6	7	8	9
10	11	12	13	14	15	16
17	18	19	20	21	22	23
24	25	26	27	28	29	30
31						

◯:3 ◑:10 ●:18 ◐:26

August

M	T	W	T	F	S	S
	1	2	3	4	5	6
7	8	9	10	11	12	13
14	15	16	17	18	19	20
21	22	23	24	25	26	27
28	29	30	31			

◯:2 ◑:8 ●:16 ◐:24 ◯:31

September

M	T	W	T	F	S	S
				1	2	3
4	5	6	7	8	9	10
11	12	13	14	15	16	17
18	19	20	21	22	23	24
25	26	27	28	29	30	

◯:7 ●:15 ◐:23 ◯:29

October

M	T	W	T	F	S	S
						1
2	3	4	5	6	7	8
9	10	11	12	13	14	15
16	17	18	19	20	21	22
23	24	25	26	27	28	29
30	31					

◑:7 ●:15 ◐:22 ◯:29

November

M	T	W	T	F	S	S
		1	2	3	4	5
6	7	8	9	10	11	12
13	14	15	16	17	18	19
20	21	22	23	24	25	26
27	28	29	30			

◑:5 ●:13 ◐:20 ◯:27

December

M	T	W	T	F	S	S
				1	2	3
4	5	6	7	8	9	10
11	12	13	14	15	16	17
18	19	20	21	22	23	24
25	26	27	28	29	30	31

◑:5 ●:13 ◐:20 ◯:27

---

1 Jan ● New Year's Day	10 Apr ● Easter Monday	22 Dec ● December Solstice
26 Jan ● Australia Day	25 Apr ● ANZAC Day	25 Dec ● Christmas Day
21 Mar ● March Equinox	22 Jun ● June Solstice	26 Dec ● Boxing Day
7 Apr ● Good Friday	23 Sep ● September Equinox	

A WONDROUS YEAR

JANUARY

FEBRUARY

MARCH

APRIL

MAY

JUNE

JULY

AUGUST

SEPTEMBER

OCTOBER

NOVEMBER

DECEMBER

End of Year Reflection

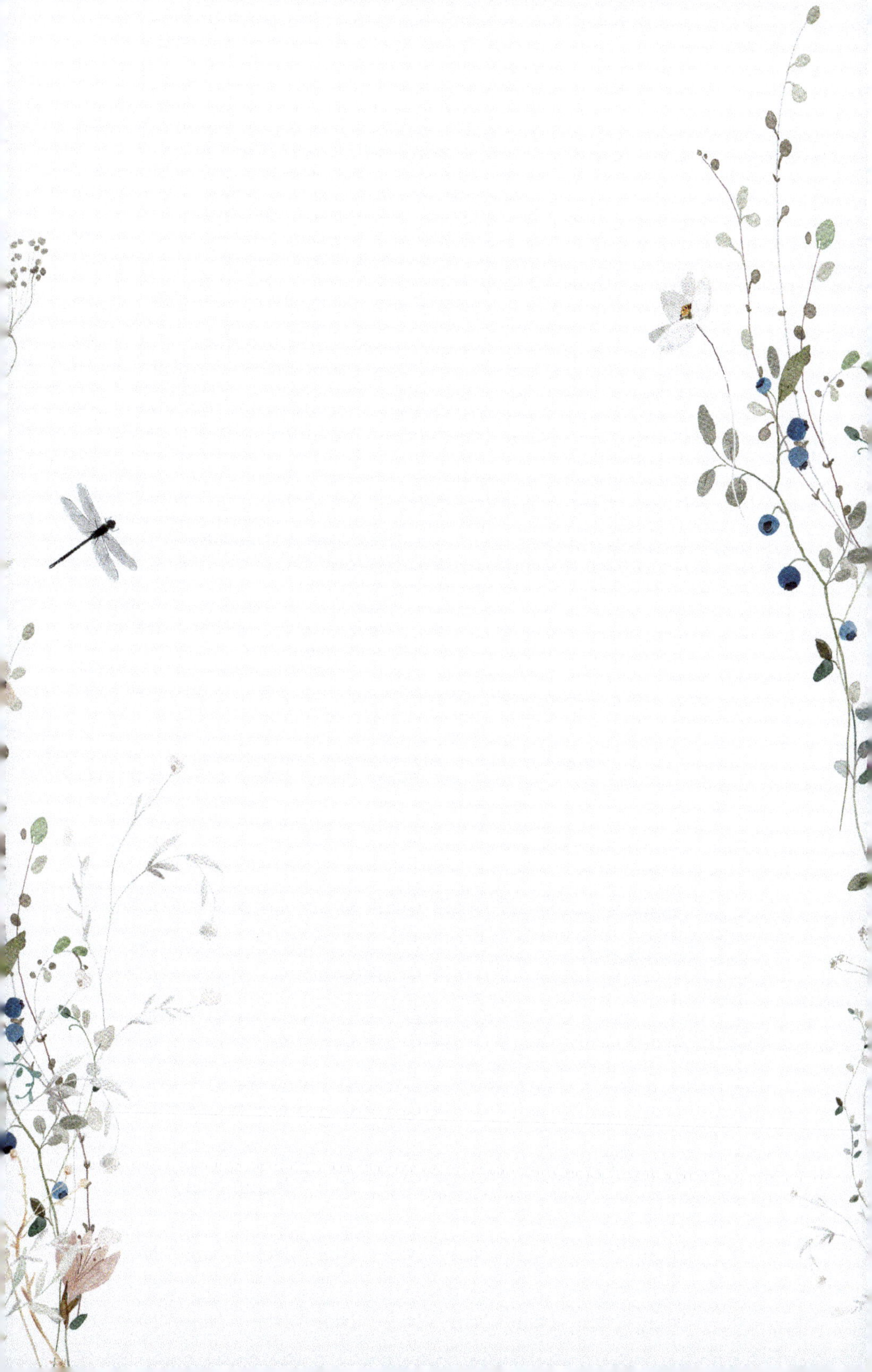

New Year

New Dreams

Moon Dates

2023

SOUTHERN HEMISPHERE

The following moon dates are on based AEST

New Moon 		Full Moon	
January	22	January	7
February	20	February	6
March	22	March	7
April	20	April	6
May	20	May	6
June	18	June	4
July	18	July	3
August	16	August	2, 31
September	15	September	29
October	15	October	29
November	13	November	27
December	13	December	27

MOON PHASES

New Moon: It's time to make a fresh start, set new intentions, sow new seeds, initiate new projects. Just keep it easy and light while the energy is still new.

Waxing Moon: The moon is growing larger, energy is rising and expanding. It's a good time for brainstorming, planning and taking actions. Perfect for creating momentum or trying something new.

Full Moon: The moon is full in the sky, energy is peaking and it's time to be seen or heard. Great time to make an announcement, launch or pitch a project/product and connect or celebrate with others.

Waning Moon: The moon is growing smaller in the sky. Energy is reducing and signaling a time to finish up loose ends and complete the work you have in hand.

Balsamic Moon: "Balsamic" means healing and soothing. As the moon continues to grow smaller, it's time to make peace with where you are and appreciate all the blessings in your life. Trust in divine timing.

Dark Moon: This is the day before new moon begins. It's a good time to rest and reflect. You may feel you need a bath or go to bed early. Slow down and relax.

the future belongs to those who believe in the beauty of their dreams.

-Eleanor Roosevelt

JANUARY

SUN	MON	TUE	WED	THU	FRI	SAT
1	2	3	4	5	6	7
8	9	10	11	12	13	14
15	16	17	18	19	20	21
22	23	24	25	26	27	28
29	30	31				

GOALS THIS MONTH:

Weekly Planner

MOON PHASE: NEW MOON / WAXING / FULL MOON / WANING

GOALS THIS WEEK: **REMINDER:**

TO-DO LIST:

Happy New Year!

December 2022 / January 2023

26
MON

....

27
TUE

....

28
WED

....

29
THURS

....

30
FRI

....

31
SAT

....

1
SUN

HAPPY NEW YEAR!

....

Weekly Planner

MOON PHASE: NEW MOON / WAXING / FULL MOON / WANING

GOALS THIS WEEK:

REMINDER:

TO-DO LIST:

Weekly Schedule

January

2

MON

3

TUE

4

WED

5

THURS

6

FRI

7

SAT

8

SUN

Weekly Planner

MOON PHASE: NEW MOON / WAXING / FULL MOON / WANING

GOALS THIS WEEK:

REMINDER:

TO-DO LIST:

Weekly Schedule

January

9
MON
....

10
TUE
....

11
WED
....

12
THURS
....

13
FRI
....

14
SAT
....

15
SUN
....

Weekly Planner

MOON PHASE: NEW MOON / WAXING / FULL MOON / WANING

GOALS THIS WEEK:

REMINDER:

TO-DO LIST:

Weekly Schedule

January

16
MON

....

17
TUE

....

18
WED

....

19
THURS

....

20
FRI

....

21
SAT

....

22
SUN

....

Weekly Planner

GOALS THIS WEEK:

REMINDER:

TO-DO LIST:

Weekly Schedule

23
MON

....

24
TUE

....

25
WED

....

26
THURS

....

27
FRI

....

28
SAT

....

29
SUN

....

Weekly Planner

MOON PHASE: NEW MOON / WAXING / FULL MOON / WANING

GOALS THIS WEEK:

REMINDER:

TO-DO LIST:

Weekly Schedule

anuary/Feburary

30
MON
....

31
TUE
....

1
WED
....

2
THURS
....

3
FRI
....

4
SAT
....

5
SUN
....

FEBRUARY

SUN	MON	TUE	WED	THU	FRI	SAT
			1	2	3	4
5	6	7	8	9	10	11
12	13	14	15	16	17	18
19	20	21	22	23	24	25
26	27	28				

GOALS THIS MONTH:

Weekly Planner

GOALS THIS WEEK:

REMINDER:

TO-DO LIST:

Weekly Schedule

Feburary

6
MON
....

7
TUE
....

8
WED
....

9
THURS
....

10
FRI
....

11
SAT
....

12
SUN
....

Weekly Planner

MOON PHASE: NEW MOON / WAXING / FULL MOON / WANING

GOALS THIS WEEK:

REMINDER:

TO-DO LIST:

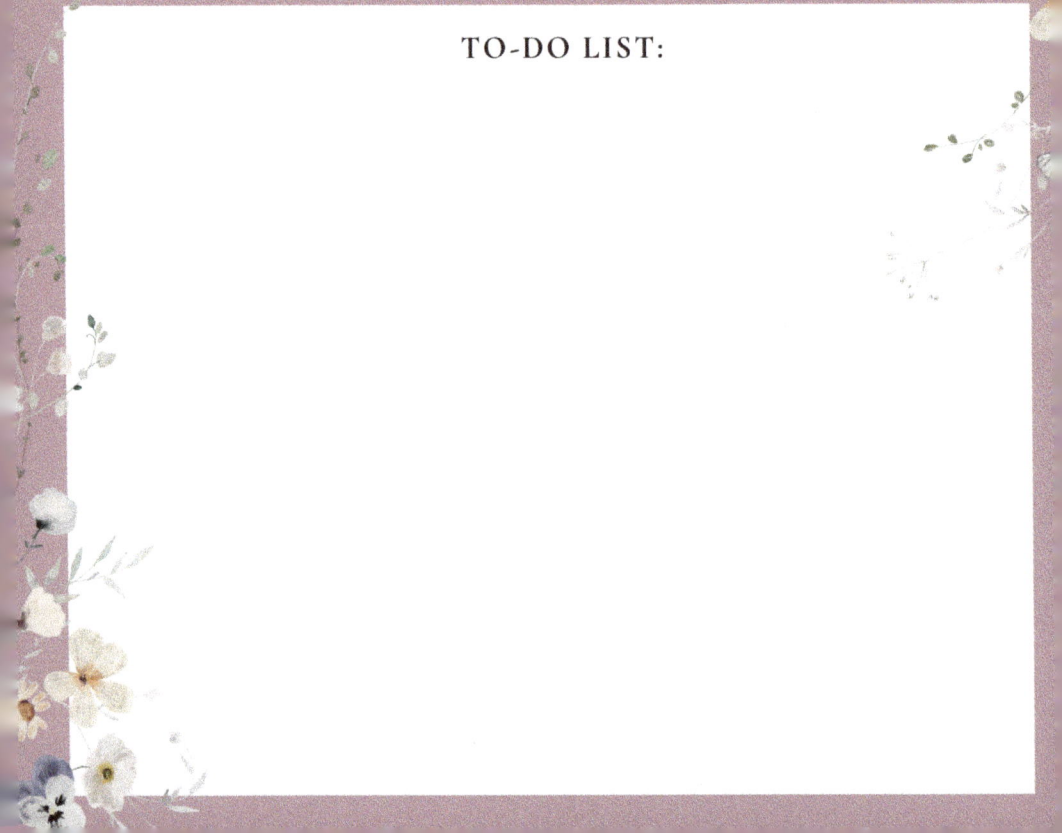

Weekly Schedule

Feburary

13
MON

....

14
TUE

....

15
WED

....

16
THURS

....

17
FRI

....

18
SAT

....

19
SUN

....

Weekly Planner

MOON PHASE: NEW MOON / WAXING / FULL MOON / WANING

GOALS THIS WEEK:

REMINDER:

TO-DO LIST:

Weekly Schedule

Feburary

20
MON

....

21
TUE

....

22
WED

....

23
THURS

....

24
FRI

....

25
SAT

....

26
SUN

....

Weekly Planner

MOON PHASE: NEW MOON / WAXING / FULL MOON / WANING

GOALS THIS WEEK:

REMINDER:

TO-DO LIST:

Weekly Schedule

Feburary / March

27
MON

....

28
TUE

....

1
WED

....

2
THURS

....

3
FRI

....

4
SAT

....

5
SUN

....

MARCH

SUN	MON	TUE	WED	THU	FRI	SAT
			1	2	3	4
5	6	7	8	9	10	11
12	13	14	15	16	17	18
19	20	21	22	23	24	25
26	27	28	29	30	31	

GOALS THIS MONTH:

Weekly Planner

MOON PHASE: NEW MOON / WAXING / FULL MOON / WANING

GOALS THIS WEEK:

REMINDER:

TO-DO LIST:

Weekly Schedule

March

6
MON
....

7
TUE
....

8
WED
....

9
THURS
....

10
FRI
....

11
SAT
....

12
SUN
....

Weekly Planner

MOON PHASE: NEW MOON / WAXING / FULL MOON / WANING

GOALS THIS WEEK:

REMINDER:

TO-DO LIST:

Weekly Schedule

March

13
MON

....

14
TUE

....

15
WED

....

16
THURS

....

17
FRI

....

18
SAT

....

19
SUN

....

Weekly Planner

MOON PHASE: NEW MOON / WAXING / FULL MOON / WANING

GOALS THIS WEEK:

REMINDER:

TO-DO LIST:

Weekly Schedule

March

20
MON

....

21
TUE

....

22
WED

....

23
THURS

....

24
FRI

....

25
SAT

....

26
SUN

....

Weekly Planner

MOON PHASE: NEW MOON / WAXING / FULL MOON / WANING

GOALS THIS WEEK:

REMINDER:

TO-DO LIST:

Weekly Schedule

March / April

27
MON

....

28
TUE

....

29
WED

....

30
THURS

....

31
FRI

....

1
SAT

....

2
SUN

....

QUARTERLY REFLECTION

APRIL

SUN	MON	TUE	WED	THU	FRI	SAT
						1
2	3	4	5	6	7	8
9	10	11	12	13	14	15
16	17	18	19	20	21	22
23 / 30	24	25	26	27	28	29

GOALS THIS MONTH:

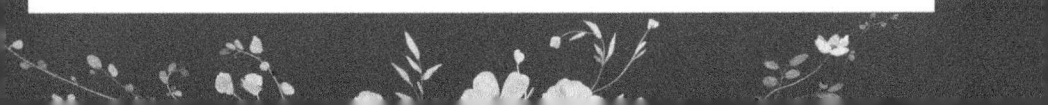

Weekly Planner

MOON PHASE: NEW MOON / WAXING / FULL MOON / WANING

GOALS THIS WEEK:

REMINDER:

TO-DO LIST:

Weekly Schedule

April

3
MON
....

4
TUE
....

5
WED
....

6
THURS
....

7
FRI
....

8
SAT
....

9
SUN
....

Weekly Planner

MOON PHASE: NEW MOON / WAXING / FULL MOON / WANING

GOALS THIS WEEK:

REMINDER:

TO-DO LIST:

Weekly Schedule

April

10
MON

....

11
TUE

....

12
WED

....

13
THURS

....

14
FRI

....

15
SAT

....

16
SUN

....

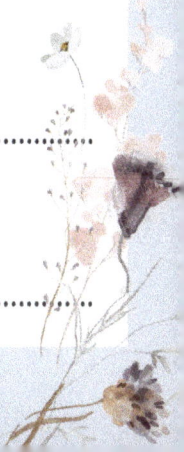

Weekly Planner

MOON PHASE: NEW MOON / WAXING / FULL MOON / WANING

GOALS THIS WEEK:

REMINDER:

TO-DO LIST:

Weekly Schedule

April

17
MON

....

18
TUE

....

19
WED

....

20
THURS

....

21
FRI

....

22
SAT

....

23
SUN

....

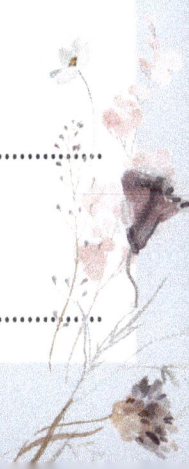

Weekly Planner

MOON PHASE: NEW MOON / WAXING / FULL MOON / WANING

GOALS THIS WEEK:

REMINDER:

TO-DO LIST:

Weekly Schedule

April

24
MON

....

25
TUE

....

26
WED

....

27
THURS

....

28
FRI

....

29
SAT

....

30
SUN

....

MAY

SUN	MON	TUE	WED	THU	FRI	SAT
	1	2	3	4	5	6
7	8	9	10	11	12	13
14	15	16	17	18	19	20
21	22	23	24	25	26	27
28	29	30	31			

GOALS THIS MONTH:

Weekly Planner

MOON PHASE: NEW MOON / WAXING / FULL MOON / WANING

GOALS THIS WEEK:

REMINDER:

TO-DO LIST:

Weekly Schedule

May

1
MON

....

2
TUE

....

3
WED

....

4
THURS

....

5
FRI

....

6
SAT

....

7
SUN

....

Weekly Planner

MOON PHASE: NEW MOON / WAXING / FULL MOON / WANING

GOALS THIS WEEK:

REMINDER:

TO-DO LIST:

Weekly Schedule

May

8
MON
....

9
TUE
....

10
WED
....

11
THURS
....

12
FRI
....

13
SAT
....

14
SUN
....

Weekly Planner

MOON PHASE: NEW MOON / WAXING / FULL MOON / WANING

GOALS THIS WEEK:

REMINDER:

TO-DO LIST:

Weekly Schedule

May

15
MON

....

16
TUE

....

17
WED

....

18
THURS

....

19
FRI

....

20
SAT

....

21
SUN

....

Weekly Planner

MOON PHASE: NEW MOON / WAXING / FULL MOON / WANING

GOALS THIS WEEK:

REMINDER:

TO-DO LIST:

Weekly Schedule

May

22
MON
....

23
TUE
....

24
WED
....

25
THURS
....

26
FRI
....

27
SAT
....

28
SUN
....

Weekly Planner

MOON PHASE: NEW MOON / WAXING / FULL MOON / WANING

GOALS THIS WEEK:

REMINDER:

TO-DO LIST:

Weekly Schedule

May / June

29
MON

....

30
TUE

....

31
WED

....

1
THURS

....

2
FRI

....

3
SAT

....

4
SUN

....

JUNE

SUN	MON	TUE	WED	THU	FRI	SAT
				1	2	3
4	5	6	7	8	9	10
11	12	13	14	15	16	17
18	19	20	21	22	23	24
25	26	27	28	29	30	

GOALS THIS MONTH:

Weekly Planner

MOON PHASE: NEW MOON / WAXING / FULL MOON / WANING

GOALS THIS WEEK: REMINDER:

TO-DO LIST:

Weekly Schedule

June

5
MON

....

6
TUE

....

7
WED

....

8
THURS

....

9
FRI

....

10
SAT

....

11
SUN

....

Weekly Planner

MOON PHASE: NEW MOON / WAXING / FULL MOON / WANING

GOALS THIS WEEK: REMINDER:

TO-DO LIST:

Weekly Schedule

June

12
MON

....

13
TUE

....

14
WED

....

15
THURS

....

16
FRI

....

17
SAT

....

18
SUN

....

Weekly Planner

MOON PHASE: NEW MOON / WAXING / FULL MOON / WANING

GOALS THIS WEEK: **REMINDER:**

TO-DO LIST:

Weekly Schedule

June

19
MON

....

20
TUE

....

21
WED

....

22
THURS

....

23
FRI

....

24
SAT

....

25
SUN

....

Weekly Planner

MOON PHASE: NEW MOON / WAXING / FULL MOON / WANING

GOALS THIS WEEK: REMINDER:

TO-DO LIST:

Weekly Schedule

June / July

26
MON

....

27
TUE

....

28
WED

....

29
THURS

....

30
FRI

....

1
SAT

....

2
SUN

....

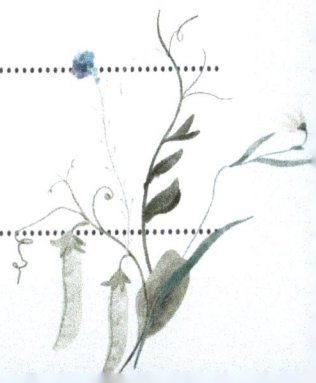

QUARTERLY REFLECTION

JULY

SUN	MON	TUE	WED	THU	FRI	SAT
						1
2	3	4	5	6	7	8
9	10	11	12	13	14	15
16	17	18	19	20	21	22
23 / 30	24 / 31	25	26	27	28	29

GOALS THIS MONTH:

Weekly Planner

MOON PHASE: NEW MOON / WAXING / FULL MOON / WANING

GOALS THIS WEEK:

REMINDER:

TO-DO LIST:

Weekly Schedule

July

3
MON

....

4
TUE

....

5
WED

....

6
THURS

....

7
FRI

....

8
SAT

....

9
SUN

....

Weekly Planner

MOON PHASE: NEW MOON / WAXING / FULL MOON / WANING

GOALS THIS WEEK:

REMINDER:

TO-DO LIST:

Weekly Schedule

July

10
MON
....

11
TUE
....

12
WED
....

13
THURS
....

14
FRI
....

15
SAT
....

16
SUN
....

Weekly Planner

MOON PHASE: NEW MOON / WAXING / FULL MOON / WANING

GOALS THIS WEEK:

REMINDER:

TO-DO LIST:

Weekly Schedule

July

17
MON

18
TUE

19
WED

20
THURS

21
FRI

22
SAT

23
SUN

Weekly Planner

MOON PHASE: NEW MOON / WAXING / FULL MOON / WANING

GOALS THIS WEEK:

REMINDER:

TO-DO LIST:

Weekly Schedule

July

24
MON
....

25
TUE
....

26
WED
....

27
THURS
....

28
FRI
....

29
SAT
....

30
SUN
....

Weekly Planner

MOON PHASE: NEW MOON / WAXING / FULL MOON / WANING

GOALS THIS WEEK:

REMINDER:

TO-DO LIST:

Weekly Schedule

July / August

31
MON

....

1

TUE

....

2
WED

....

3

THURS

....

4
FRI

....

5
SAT

....

6
SUN

....

AUGUST

SUN	MON	TUE	WED	THU	FRI	SAT
		1	2	3	4	5
6	7	8	9	10	11	12
13	14	15	16	17	18	19
20	21	22	23	24	25	26
27	28	29	30	31		

GOALS THIS MONTH:

Weekly Planner

MOON PHASE: NEW MOON / WAXING / FULL MOON / WANING

GOALS THIS WEEK: REMINDER:

TO-DO LIST:

Weekly Schedule

August

7
MON
....

8
TUE
....

9
WED
....

10
THURS
....

11
FRI
....

12
SAT
....

13
SUN
....

Weekly Planner

MOON PHASE: NEW MOON / WAXING / FULL MOON / WANING

GOALS THIS WEEK:

REMINDER:

TO-DO LIST:

Weekly Schedule

August

14
MON

....

15
TUE

....

16
WED

....

17
THURS

....

18
FRI

....

19
SAT

....

20
SUN

....

Weekly Planner

MOON PHASE: NEW MOON / WAXING / FULL MOON / WANING

GOALS THIS WEEK: REMINDER:

TO-DO LIST:

Weekly Schedule

August

21
MON

....

22
TUE

....

23
WED

....

24
THURS

....

25
FRI

....

26
SAT

....

27
SUN

....

Weekly Planner

MOON PHASE: NEW MOON / WAXING / FULL MOON / WANING

GOALS THIS WEEK: REMINDER:

TO-DO LIST:

Weekly Schedule

August / September

28
MON
....

29
TUE
....

30
WED
....

31
THURS
....

1
FRI
....

2
SAT
....

3
SUN
....

SEPTEMBER

SUN	MON	TUE	WED	THU	FRI	SAT
					1	2
3	4	5	6	7	8	9
10	11	12	13	14	15	16
17	18	19	20	21	22	23
24	25	26	27	28	29	30

GOALS THIS MONTH:

Weekly Planner

MOON PHASE: NEW MOON / WAXING / FULL MOON / WANING

GOALS THIS WEEK:

REMINDER:

TO-DO LIST:

Weekly Schedule

September

4
MON

....

5
TUE

....

6
WED

....

7
THURS

....

8
FRI

....

9
SAT

....

10
SUN

....

Weekly Planner

MOON PHASE: NEW MOON / WAXING / FULL MOON / WANING

GOALS THIS WEEK:

REMINDER:

TO-DO LIST:

Weekly Schedule

September

11
MON

....

12
TUE

....

13
WED

....

14
THURS

....

15
FRI

....

16
SAT

....

17
SUN

....

Weekly Planner

MOON PHASE: NEW MOON / WAXING / FULL MOON / WANING

GOALS THIS WEEK:

REMINDER:

TO-DO LIST:

Weekly Schedule

September

18
MON

....

19
TUE

....

20
WED

....

21
THURS

....

22
FRI

....

23
SAT

....

24
SUN

....

Weekly Planner

MOON PHASE: NEW MOON / WAXING / FULL MOON / WANING

GOALS THIS WEEK: REMINDER:

TO-DO LIST:

Weekly Schedule

September / October

25
MON

....

26
TUE

....

27
WED

....

28
THURS

....

29
FRI

....

30
SAT

....

1
SUN

....

QUARTERLY REFLECTION

OCTOBER

SUN	MON	TUE	WED	THU	FRI	SAT
1	2	3	4	5	6	7
8	9	10	11	12	13	14
15	16	17	18	19	20	21
22	23	24	25	26	27	28
29	30	31				

GOALS THIS MONTH:

Weekly Planner

MOON PHASE: NEW MOON / WAXING / FULL MOON / WANING

GOALS THIS WEEK:

REMINDER:

TO-DO LIST:

Weekly Schedule

October

2
MON
....

3
TUE
....

4
WED
....

5
THURS
....

6
FRI
....

7
SAT
....

8
SUN
....

Weekly Planner

MOON PHASE: NEW MOON / WAXING / FULL MOON / WANING

GOALS THIS WEEK:

REMINDER:

TO-DO LIST:

Weekly Schedule

October

9
MON
....

10
TUE
....

11
WED
....

12
THURS
....

13
FRI
....

14
SAT
....

15
SUN
....

Weekly Planner

MOON PHASE: NEW MOON / WAXING / FULL MOON / WANING

GOALS THIS WEEK:

REMINDER:

TO-DO LIST:

Weekly Schedule

October

16
MON
....

17
TUE
....

18
WED
....

19
THURS
....

20
FRI
....

21
SAT
....

22
SUN
....

Weekly Planner

MOON PHASE: NEW MOON / WAXING / FULL MOON / WANING

GOALS THIS WEEK:

REMINDER:

TO-DO LIST:

Weekly Schedule

October

23
MON
....

24
TUE
....

25
WED
....

26
THURS
....

27
FRI
....

28
SAT
....

29
SUN
....

Weekly Planner

MOON PHASE: NEW MOON / WAXING / FULL MOON / WANING

GOALS THIS WEEK:

REMINDER:

TO-DO LIST:

Weekly Schedule

October / November

30
MON
....

31
TUE
....

1
WED
....

2
THURS
....

3
FRI
....

4
SAT
....

5
SUN
....

NOVEMBER

SUN	MON	TUE	WED	THU	FRI	SAT
			1	2	3	4
5	6	7	8	9	10	11
12	13	14	15	16	17	18
19	20	21	22	23	24	25
26	27	28	29	30		

GOALS THIS MONTH:

Weekly Planner

MOON PHASE: NEW MOON / WAXING / FULL MOON / WANING

GOALS THIS WEEK:

REMINDER:

TO-DO LIST:

Weekly Schedule

November

6
MON
....

7
TUE
....

8
WED
....

9
THURS
....

10
FRI
....

11
SAT
....

12
SUN
....

Weekly Planner

MOON PHASE: NEW MOON / WAXING / FULL MOON / WANING

GOALS THIS WEEK:

REMINDER:

TO-DO LIST:

Weekly Schedule

November

13
MON

....

14
TUE

....

15
WED

....

16
THURS

....

17
FRI

....

18
SAT

....

19
SUN

....

Weekly Planner

MOON PHASE: NEW MOON / WAXING / FULL MOON / WANING

GOALS THIS WEEK:

REMINDER:

TO-DO LIST:

Weekly Schedule

November

20
MON

....

21
TUE

....

22
WED

....

23
THURS

....

24
FRI

....

25
SAT

....

26
SUN

....

Weekly Planner

MOON PHASE: NEW MOON / WAXING / FULL MOON / WANING

GOALS THIS WEEK:

REMINDER:

TO-DO LIST:

Weekly Schedule

November / December

27
MON

....

28
TUE

....

29
WED

....

30
THURS

....

1
FRI

....

2
SAT

....

3
SUN

....

Merry Christmas

DECEMBER

SUN	MON	TUE	WED	THU	FRI	SAT
					1	2
3	4	5	6	7	8	9
10	11	12	13	14	15	16
17	18	19	20	21	22	23
24 / 31	25	26	27	28	29	30

Weekly Planner

MOON PHASE: NEW MOON / WAXING / FULL MOON / WANING

GOALS THIS WEEK:

REMINDER:

TO-DO LIST:

Weekly Schedule

December

4

MON

....

5

TUE

....

6

WED

....

7

THURS

....

8

FRI

....

9

SAT

....

10

SUN

....

Weekly Planner

MOON PHASE: NEW MOON / WAXING / FULL MOON / WANING

GOALS THIS WEEK:

REMINDER:

TO-DO LIST:

Weekly Schedule

December

11
MON

....

12
TUE

....

13
WED

....

14
THURS

....

15
FRI

....

16
SAT

....

17
SUN

....

Weekly Planner

MOON PHASE: NEW MOON / WAXING / FULL MOON / WANING

GOALS THIS WEEK:

REMINDER:

TO-DO LIST:

Weekly Schedule

December

18
MON
....

19
TUE
....

20
WED
....

21
THURS
....

22
FRI
....

23
SAT
....

24
SUN
....

Weekly Planner

MOON PHASE: NEW MOON / WAXING / FULL MOON / WANING

GOALS THIS WEEK:

REMINDER:

TO-DO LIST:

Weekly Schedule

December

25
MON

....

26
TUE

....

27
WED

....

28
THURS

....

29
FRI

....

30
SAT

....

31
SUN

....

Merry Christmas

the things I am grateful for this year ...

*We don't see things as they are,
we see them as we are.*

Anais Nin

About Sze Wing Vetault

Sze Wing is a coach, author and creative entrepreneur. She works with career women, busy mums and purpose-driven business owners to create more authentic success in their lives. She helps women to uncover their feminine wisdom to find more joy, fulfilment and purpose in life.

With a background in Economics (BSc.) and Political Sciences (MSc.), she has built a diverse career as a business consultant for private and public companies in education and media.

Sze Wing speaks at events and workshops. She runs a podcast and teaches courses online and in person. She works with entrepreneurs to publish their non-fiction books and other creative products. She is also a mum to two young children.

She loves yoga, dancing and travelling with her family. She is based in Sydney, Australia.

For more information, please visit her website at:
www.SzeWingVetault.com